6 Full-Length Georgia Milestones Assessment System Grade 3 Math Practice Tests

Extra Test Prep to Help Ace the GMAS Grade 3 Math Test

By

Michael Smith & Reza Nazari

6 Full-Length Georgia Milestones Assessment System Grade 3 Math Practice Tests

Published in the United State of America By

The Math Notion

Web: WWW.MathNotion.Com

Email: info@Mathnotion.com

About the Author

Michael Smith has been a math instructor for over a decade now. He holds a master's degree in Management. Since 2006, Michael has devoted his time to both teaching and developing exceptional math learning materials. As a Math instructor and test prep expert, Michael has worked with thousands of students. He has used the feedback of his students to develop a unique study program that can be used by students to drastically improve their math score fast and effectively.

– SAT Math Practice Book

– ACT Math Practice Book

– GRE Math Practice Book

– Common Core Math Practice Book

–many Math Education Workbooks, Exercise Books and Study Guides

As an experienced Math teacher, Mr. Smith employs a variety of formats to help students achieve their goals: He tutors online and in person, he teaches students in large groups, and he provides training materials and textbooks through his website and through Amazon.

You can contact Michael via email at:

info@Mathnotion.com

Prepare for the Georgia Milestones Assessment System Grade 3 Math test with a perfect practice book!

The surest way to practice your GMAS Math test-taking skills is with simulated exams. This comprehensive practice book with 6 full length and realistic GMAS Math practice tests help you measure your exam readiness, find your weak areas, and succeed on the GMAS Math test. The detailed answers and explanations for each GMAS Math question help you master every aspect of the GMAS Math.

6 Full-length Georgia Milestones Assessment System Grade 3 Math Practice Tests is a prestigious resource to help you succeed on the GMAS Math test. This perfect practice book features:

- Content 100% aligned with the GMAS test
- Six full-length GMAS Math practice tests similar to the actual test in length, format, question types, and degree of difficulty
- Detailed answers and explanations for the GMAS Math practice questions
- Written by GMAS Math top instructors and experts

After completing this hands-on exercise book, you will gain confidence, strong foundation, and adequate practice to succeed on the GMAS Math test.

WWW.MathNotion.COM

… So Much More Online!

✓ FREE Math Lessons

✓ More Math Learning Books!

✓ Mathematics Worksheets

✓ Online Math Tutors

For a PDF Version of This Book

Please Visit WWW.MathNotion.com

Contents

GMAS Math Practice Tests

Time to Test

Time to refine your skill with a practice examination

Take a REAL GMAS Mathematics test to simulate the test day experience. After you've finished, score your test using the answer key.

Before You Start

- You'll need a pencil and scratch papers to take the test.

- For this practice test, don't time yourself. Spend time as much as you need.

- It's okay to guess. You won't lose any points if you're wrong.

- After you've finished the test, review the answer key to see where you went wrong.

Calculators are not permitted for Grade 3 GMAS Tests

Good Luck!

GMAS GRADE 3 MAHEMATICS REFRENCE MATERIALS

LENGTH

Customary	Metric
1 mile (mi) = 1,760 yards (yd)	1 kilometer (km) = 1,000 meters (m)
1 yard (yd) = 3 feet (ft)	1 meter (m) = 100 centimeters (cm)
1 foot (ft) = 12 inches (in.)	1 centimeter (cm) = 10 millimeters (mm)

VOLUME AND CAPACITY

Customary	Metric
1 gallon (gal) = 4 quarts (qt)	1 liter (L) = 1,000 milliliters (mL)
1 quart (qt) = 2 pints (pt.)	
1 pint (pt.) = 2 cups (c)	
1 cup (c) = 8 fluid ounces (Fl oz)	

WEIGHT AND MASS

Customary	Metric
1 ton (T) = 2,000 pounds (lb.)	1 kilogram (kg) = 1,000 grams (g)
1 pound (lb.) = 16 ounces (oz)	1 gram (g) = 1,000 milligrams (mg)

Time

1 year = 12 months

1 year = 52 weeks

1 week = 7 days

1 day = 24 hours

1 hour = 60 minutes

1 minute = 60 seconds

Georgia Milestones Assessment

System Practice Test 1

Mathematics

GRADE 3

Administered Month Year

Session 1

❖ **Calculators are NOT permitted for this practice test.**

❖ **Time for Session 1: 85 Minutes**

1) There are 2 days in a weekend. There are 24 hours in day. How many hours are in a weekend?

   A. 48

   B. 96

   C. 168

   D. 200

2) This clock shows a time after 12:00 PM. What time was it 1 hours and 45 minutes ago?

   A. 12:45 PM

   B. 1:45 PM

   C. 1: 15 PM

   D. 12:30 PM

3) A football team is buying new uniforms. Each uniform cost $30. The team wants to buy 12uniforms.

   Which equation represents a way to find the total cost of the uniforms?

   A. $(30 \times 10) + (1 \times 12) = 300 + 12$

   B. $(30 \times 10) + (10 \times 1) = 300 + 10$

   C. $(30 \times 10) + (30 \times 2) = 300 + 60$

   D. $(12 \times 10) + (10 \times 20) = 120 + 200$

4) Olivia has 93 pastilles. She wants to put them in boxes of 3 pastilles. How many boxes does she need?

Write your answer in the box below.

5) Mia's goal is to save $160 to purchase her favorite bike.

- In January, she saved $46.

- In February, she saved $38.

How much money does Mia need to save in March to be able to purchase her favorite bike?

A. $28

B. $30

C. $52

D. $76

6) Michelle has 84 old books. She plans to send all of them to the library in their area. If she puts the books in boxes which can hold 4 books, which of the following equations can be used to find the number of boxes she will use?

A. $84 + 4 =$ _____

B. $84 \times 4 =$ _____

C. $84 - 4 =$ _____

D. $84 \div 4 =$ _____

7) Elise had 956 cards. Then, she gave 352 of the cards to her friend Alice. After

that, Elise lost 250 cards.

Which equation can be used to find the number of cards Elise has now?

A. $956 - 352 + 250 = $ _____

B. $956 - 352 - 250 = $ _____

C. $956 + 352 + 250 = $ _____

D. $956 + 352 - 250 = $ _____

8) The length of the following rectangle is 9 centimeters and its width is 4

centimeters. What is the area of the rectangle?

A. 12 cm^2

B. 21 cm^2

C. 36 cm^2

D. 22 cm^2

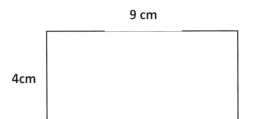

9) Look at the spinner above. On which color is the spinner most likely to land?

A. Red

B. Green

C. Yellow

D. None

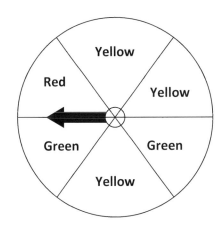

10) A group of third grade students recorded the following distances that they jumped.

23 inches	36 inches	24 inches	28 inches
36 inches	33 inches	25 inches	34 inches
32 inches	28 inches	34 inches	36 inches

What is the distance that was jumped most often?

A. 23

B. 24

C. 32

D. 36

Session 2

❖ **Calculators are NOT permitted for this practice test.**

❖ **Time for Session 2: 85 Minutes**

11) A number sentence such as $25 + Z = 92$ can be called an equation. If this equation is true, then which of the following equations is not true?

A. $92 - 25 = Z$

B. $92 - Z = 25$

C. $Z - 92 = 25$

D. $Z = 67$

12) Which number correctly completes the number sentence $80 \times 35 =$?

A. 350

B. 900

C. 1,250

D. 2,800

13) Which of the following statements describes the number 26,586?

A. The sum of two thousands, 6 thousands, five hundreds, eighty tens, and six ones

B. The sum of sixty thousands, 2 thousands, five hundreds, eight tens, and six ones

C. The sum of twenty thousands, 6 thousands, fifty hundreds, eighty tens, and six ones

D. The sum of twenty thousands, 6 thousands, five hundreds, eight tens, and six ones

14) Use the models below to answer the question.

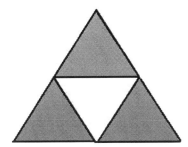 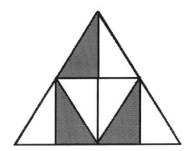

Which statement about the models is true?

A. Each shows the same fraction because they are the same size.

B. Each shows a different fraction because they are different shapes.

C. Each shows the same fraction because they both have 3 sections shaded.

D. Each shows a different fraction because they both have 3 shaded sections but a different number of total sections.

15) Classroom A contains 7 rows of chairs with 5 chairs per row. If classroom B has three times as many chairs, which number sentence can be used to find the number of chairs in classroom B?

A. $7 \times 5 + 3$

B. $7 + 5 \times 3$

C. $7 \times 5 \times 3$

D. $7 + 5 + 3$

16) Which number correctly completes the subtraction sentence

$7000 - 858 = $ _____ ?

A. 6,142

B. 7,452

C. 742

D. 7,458

17) A cafeteria menu had spaghetti with meatballs for $8 and bean soup for $7 How much would it cost to buy three plates of spaghetti with meatballs and three bowls of bean soup?

Write your answer in the box below.

18) Emma flew 3,391 miles from Los Angeles to New York City. What is the number of miles Emma flew rounded to the nearest thousand?

A. 2,000

B. 2,400

C. 2,500

D. 3,000

19) To what number is the arrow pointing?

A. 24

8   20   36

22

B. 28

C. 30

D. 32

20) Jason packs 12 boxes with flashcards. Each box holds 30 flashcards. How many flashcards Jason can pack into these boxes?

A. 86

B. 860

C. 530

D. 360

"This is the end of the practice test 1"

Georgia Milestones Assessment

System Practice Test 2

Mathematics

GRADE 3

Administered Month Year

Session 1

❖ **Calculators are NOT permitted for this practice test.**

❖ **Time for Session 1: 85 Minutes**

1) Kayla has 120 red cards and 85 white cards. How many more red cards than white cards do Kayla have?

    A. 17

    B. 19

    C. 35

    D. 27

2) A number sentence is shown below.

$3 \times 5 \,\square\, 8 = 120$

What symbol goes into the box to make the number sentence true?

    A. $\times$

    B. $\div$

    C. $+$

    D. $-$

3) Liam had 835 marbles. Then, he gave 432 of the cards to his friend Ethan. After that, Liam lost 116 cards.

Which equation can be used to find the number of cards Eve has now?

    A. $835 - 432 + 116 = \underline{\quad\quad}$

    B. $835 - 432 - 116 = \underline{\quad\quad}$

    C. $835 + 432 + 116 = \underline{\quad\quad}$

    D. $835 + 432 - 116 = \underline{\quad\quad}$

4) What is the value of "B" in the following equation?

$$43 + B + 7 = 63$$

A. 16

B. 18

C. 22

D. 13

5) There are two different cards on the table.

- There are 3 rows that have 12 red cards in each row.

- There are 21 white cards.

How many cards are there on the table?

A. 25

B. 57

C. 33

D. 99

6) Which of the following list shows only fractions that are equivalent to $\frac{1}{3}$?

A. $\frac{3}{9}, \frac{5}{15}, \frac{24}{72}$

B. $\frac{6}{12}, \frac{5}{15}, \frac{9}{27}$

C. $\frac{3}{9}, \frac{4}{15}, \frac{6}{18}$

D. $\frac{3}{9}, \frac{5}{10}, \frac{8}{24}$

7) What mixed number is shown by the shaded rectangles?

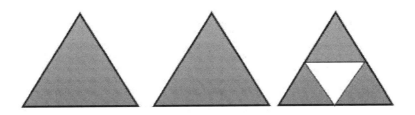

Write your answer in the box below.

┌─────────────────────┐
│   │
└─────────────────────┘

8) Mason is 15 months now and he usually eats four meals a day. How many meals does he eat in a week?

   A. 36

   B. 40

   C. 28

   D. 48

9) The perimeter of a square is 32units. Each side of this square is the same length.

   What is the length of one side of the square in units?

   A. 4

   B. 5

   C. 6

   D. 8

10) Which of the following comparison of fractions is true?

A. $\frac{3}{5} = \frac{9}{15}$

B. $\frac{2}{5} > \frac{4}{10}$

C. $\frac{2}{5} < \frac{4}{10}$

D. $\frac{2}{5} < \frac{2}{10}$

Session 2

❖ **Calculators are NOT permitted for this practice test.**

❖ **Time for Session 2: 85 Minutes**

11) What is the perimeter of this rectangle?

    A. 12 cm

    B. 24 cm

    C. 32 cm

    D. 64 cm

7 cm

5 cm

12) Nicole has 3 quarters, 5 dimes, and 4 pennies. How much money does Nicole have?

    A. 155 pennies

    B. 129 pennies

    C. 255 pennies

    D. 265 pennies

13) Noah packs 16 boxes with crayons. Each box holds 30 crayons. How many crayons Noah can pack into these boxes?

    A. 480

    B. 540

    C. 680

    D. 720

14) There are 60 minutes in an hour. How many minutes are in 5 hours?

    A. 300 minutes

    B. 320 minutes

    C. 360 minutes

    D. 400 minutes

15) There are 8 rows of chairs in a classroom with 7chairs in each row. How many chairs are in the classroom?

    A. 45

    B. 56

    C. 54

    D. 63

16) Which number correctly completes the number sentence $52 \times 14 =$?

    A. 550

    B. 660

    C. 728

    D. 990

17) Michael has 845 marbles. What is this number rounded to the nearest ten?

    Write your answer in the box below.

18) The sum of 4 ten thousand, 7 hundred, and 8 tens can be expressed as what number in standard form?

   A. 4,780

   B. 40,780

   C. 40,078

   D. 40,708

19) What is the perimeter of the following triangle?

   A. 28 inches

   B. 35 inches

   C. 48 inches

   D. 183 inches

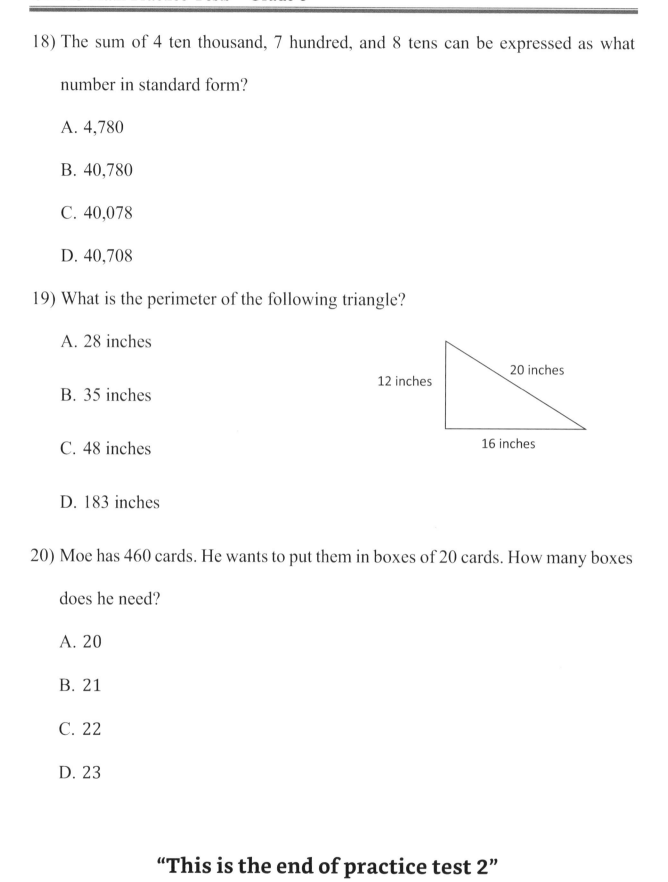

20) Moe has 460 cards. He wants to put them in boxes of 20 cards. How many boxes does he need?

   A. 20

   B. 21

   C. 22

   D. 23

"This is the end of practice test 2"

Georgia Milestones Assessment

System Practice Test 3

Mathematics

GRADE 3

Administered *Month Year*

Session 1

❖ **Calculators are NOT permitted for this practice test.**

❖ **Time for Session 1: 85 Minutes**

1) There are 3 days in a weekend. There are 24 hours in day. How many hours are in a weekend?

   A. 72

   B. 48

   C. 96

   D. 27

2) This clock shows a time after 2:15 PM. What time was it 3 hours and 25 minutes ago?

   A. 10:35 PM

   B. 11:50 PM

   C. 11:15 PM

   D. 10:50 AM

3) A football team is buying new uniforms. Each uniform cost $20. The team wants to buy 14uniforms.

   Which equation represents a way to find the total cost of the uniforms?

   A. $(20 \times 10) + (1 \times 14) = 200 + 14$

   B. $(20 \times 10) + (10 \times 1) = 200 + 10$

   C. $(20 \times 10) + (20 \times 4) = 200 + 80$

   D. $(14 \times 10) + (10 \times 20) = 140 + 200$

4) Olivia has 136 pastilles. She wants to put them in boxes of 4 pastilles. How many boxes does she need?

Write your answer in the box below.

☐

5) Mia's goal is to save $143 to purchase her favorite bike.

- In January, she saved $37.

- In February, she saved $61.

How much money does Mia need to save in March to be able to purchase her favorite bike?

A. $38

B. $35

C. $54

D. $45

6) Michelle has 65 old books. She plans to send all of them to the library in their area. If she puts the books in boxes which can hold 3 books, which of the following equations can be used to find the number of boxes she will use?

A. $65 + 3 = \underline{\hspace{1cm}}$

B. $65 \times 3 = \underline{\hspace{1cm}}$

C. $65 - 3 = \underline{\hspace{1cm}}$

D. $65 \div 3 = \underline{\hspace{1cm}}$

7) Elise had 692 cards. Then, she gave 328 of the cards to her friend Alice. After that, Elise lost 213 cards.

Which equation can be used to find the number of cards Elise has now?

A. $692 - 328 + 213 =$ _____

B. $692 - 328 - 213 =$ _____

C. $692 + 328 + 213 =$ _____

D. $692 + 328 - 213 =$ _____

8) The length of the following rectangle is 7 centimeters and its width is 5 centimeters. What is the area of the rectangle?

A. 12 cm²

B. 24 cm²

C. 35 cm²

D. 38 cm²

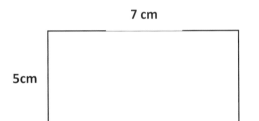

9) Look at the spinner above. On which color is the spinner most likely to land?

A. Yellow

B. Green

C. Red

D. None

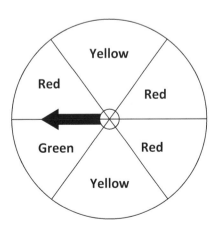

10) A group of third grade students recorded the following distances that they jumped.

13 inches	26 inches	14 inches	18 inches
26 inches	23 inches	15 inches	24 inches
22 inches	18 inches	24 inches	26 inches

What is the distance that was jumped most often?

A. 13

B. 14

C. 22

D. 26

Session 2

❖ **Calculators are NOT permitted for this practice test.**

❖ **Time for Session 2: 85 Minutes**

11) A number sentence such as $31 + Z = 86$ can be called an equation. If this equation is true, then which of the following equations is not true?

A. $86 - 31 = Z$

B. $86 - Z = 31$

C. $Z - 86 = 31$

D. $Z = 55$

12) Which number correctly completes the number sentence $60 \times 42 =$?

A. 250

B. 1,250

C. 2,250

D. 2,520

13) Which of the following statements describes the number 63,425?

A. The sum of six thousands, 3 thousands, four hundreds, twenty tens, and five ones

B. The sum of six thousands, 3 thousands, four hundreds, two tens, and five ones

C. The sum of sixty thousands, 5 thousands, four hundreds, twenty tens, and five ones

D. The sum of sixty thousands, 3 thousands, four hundreds, two tens, and five ones

14) Use the models below to answer the question.

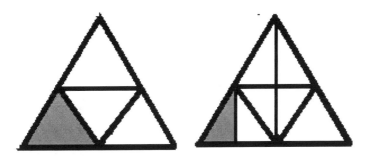

Which statement about the models is true?

A. Each shows the same fraction because they are the same size.

B. Each shows a different fraction because they are different shapes.

C. Each shows the same fraction because they both have 1 sections shaded.

D. Each shows a different fraction because they both have 1 shaded sections but a different number of total sections.

15) Classroom A contains 9 rows of chairs with 6 chairs per row. If classroom B has two times as many chairs, which number sentence can be used to find the number of chairs in classroom B?

A. $9 \times 6 + 2$

B. $9 + 6 \times 2$

C. $9 \times 6 \times 2$

D. $9 + 6 + 2$

16) Which number correctly completes the subtraction sentence

$8,000 - 1,980 = $ _____ ?

A. 6,020

B. 7,022

C. 602

D. 6,002

17) A cafeteria menu had spaghetti with meatballs for $9 and bean soup for $6 How much would it cost to buy two plates of spaghetti with meatballs and two bowls of bean soup?

Write your answer in the box below.

18) Emma flew 7,293 miles from Los Angeles to New York City. What is the number of miles Emma flew rounded to the nearest thousand?

A. 6,000

B. 6,300

C. 6,500

D. 7,000

19) To what number is the arrow pointing?

A. 22

B. 20

C. 30

D. 10

20) Jason packs 24 boxes with flashcards. Each box holds 15 flashcards. How many flashcards Jason can pack into these boxes?

A. 39

B. 240

C. 380

D. 360

"This is the end of the practice test 3"

Georgia Milestones Assessment

System Practice Test 4

Mathematics

GRADE 3

Administered *Month Year*

Session 1

❖ **Calculators are NOT permitted for this practice test.**

❖ **Time for Session 1: 85 Minutes**

1) Kayla has 155 red cards and 95 white cards. How many more reds cards than white cards do Kayla have?

   A. 50

   B. 65

   C. 60

   D. 55

2) A number sentence is shown below.

   $6 \times 7 \square 5 = 210$

   What symbol goes into the box to make the number sentence true?

   A. ×

   B. ÷

   C. +

   D. −

3) Liam had 548 marbles. Then, he gave 241 of the cards to his friend Ethan. After that, Liam lost 86 cards.

   Which equation can be used to find the number of cards Eve has now?

   A. $548 - 241 + 86 =$

   B. $548 - 241 - 86 =$

   C. $548 + 241 + 86 =$

   D. $548 + 241 - 86 =$

4) What is the value of "B" in the following equation?

$$38 + B + 16 = 77$$

    A. 26

    B. 28

    C. 32

    D. 23

5) There are two different cards on the table.

    - There are 5 rows that have 14 red cards in each row.

    - There are 23 white cards.

How many cards are there on the table?

    A. 75

    B. 93

    C. 39

    D. 96

6) Which of the following list shows only fractions that are equivalent to $\frac{1}{5}$?

    A. $\frac{3}{15}, \frac{5}{25}, \frac{24}{120}$

    B. $\frac{6}{12}, \frac{5}{25}, \frac{9}{45}$

    C. $\frac{3}{15}, \frac{4}{16}, \frac{24}{120}$

    D. $\frac{3}{15}, \frac{5}{10}, \frac{8}{40}$

7) What mixed number is shown by the shaded triangles?

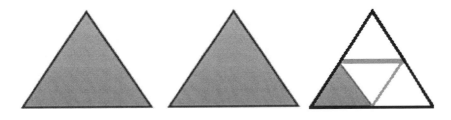

Write your answer in the box below.

8) Mason is 15 months now and he usually eats two meals a day. How many meals does he eat in a week?

A. 28

B. 21

C. 14

D. 12

9) The perimeter of a square is 44 units. Each side of this square is the same length. What is the length of one side of the square in units?

A. 8

B. 3

C. 9

D. 11

10) Which of the following comparison of fractions is true?

A. $\frac{3}{8} = \frac{9}{24}$

B. $\frac{4}{7} > \frac{8}{14}$

C. $\frac{4}{7} < \frac{8}{14}$

D. $\frac{4}{7} < \frac{2}{14}$

Session 2

❖ **Calculators are NOT permitted for this practice test.**

❖ **Time for Session 2: 85 Minutes**

11) What is the perimeter of this rectangle?

   A. 18 cm

   B. 36 cm

   C. 28 cm

   D. 80 cm

10 cm

8 cm

12) Nicole has 2 quarters, 9 dimes, and 12 pennies. How much money does Nicole

have?

   A. 140 pennies

   B. 152 pennies

   C. 125 pennies

   D. 250 pennies

13) Noah packs 19 boxes with crayons. Each box holds 20 crayons. How many

crayons Noah can pack into these boxes?

   A. 380

   B. 580

   C. 650

   D. 320

14) There are 60 minutes in an hour. How many minutes are in 4 hours?

 A. 240 minutes

 B. 420 minutes

 C. 320 minutes

 D. 460 minutes

15) There are 9 rows of chairs in a classroom with 5 chairs in each row. How many

 chairs are in the classroom?

 A. 55

 B. 45

 C. 54

 D. 60

16) Which number correctly completes the number sentence 48 × 15 =?

 A. 520

 B. 640

 C. 720

 D. 950

17) Michael has 958 marbles. What is this number rounded to the nearest ten?

 Write your answer in the box below.

18) The sum of 5 ten thousand, 3 hundred, and 4 tens can be expressed as what number in standard form?

    A. 5,340

    B. 50,340

    C. 50,034

    D. 50,304

19) What is the perimeter of the following triangle?

    A. 21 inches

    B. 54 inches

    C. 36 inches

    D. 157 inches

9 inches 15 inches 12 inches

20) Moe has 630 cards. He wants to put them in boxes of 30 cards. How many boxes does he need?

    A. 19

    B. 24

    C. 22

    D. 21

"This is the end of practice test 4"

Georgia Milestones Assessment

System Practice Test 5

Mathematics

GRADE 3

Administered *Month Year*

Session 1

❖ **Calculators are NOT permitted for this practice test.**

❖ **Time for Session 1: 85 Minutes**

1) There are 7 days in a weekend. There are 24 hours in day. How many hours are in a weekend?

A. 168

B. 188

C. 128

D. 316

2) This clock shows a time after 8:15 PM. What time was it 4 hours and 20 minutes ago?

A. 4:05 PM

B. 2:55 PM

C. 3:25 PM

D. 3:55 PM

3) A football team is buying new uniforms. Each uniform cost $30. The team wants to buy 11 uniforms.

Which equation represents a way to find the total cost of the uniforms?

A. $(30 \times 10) + (1 \times 11) = 300 + 11$

B. $(30 \times 10) + (10 \times 1) = 300 + 10$

C. $(30 \times 10) + (30 \times 1) = 300 + 30$

D. $(11 \times 10) + (10 \times 30) = 110 + 300$

4) Olivia has 82 pastilles. She wants to put them in boxes of 2 pastilles. How many boxes does she need?

Write your answer in the box below.

5) Mia's goal is to save $76 to purchase her favorite bike.

   - In January, she saved $23.

   - In February, she saved $14.

   How much money does Mia need to save in March to be able to purchase her favorite bike?

   A. $28

   B. $39

   C. $34

   D. $29

6) Michelle has 45 old books. She plans to send all of them to the library in their area. If she puts the books in boxes which can hold 5 books, which of the following equations can be used to find the number of boxes she will use?

   A. $45 + 5 =$ _____

   B. $45 \times 5 =$ _____

   C. $45 - 5 =$ _____

   D. $45 \div 5 =$ _____

7) Elise had 98 cards. Then, she gave 54 of the cards to her friend Alice. After that, Elise lost 13 cards.

Which equation can be used to find the number of cards Elise has now?

A. $98 - 54 + 13 =$ _____

B. $98 - 54 - 13 =$ _____

C. $98 + 54 + 13 =$ _____

D. $98 + 54 - 13 =$ _____

8) The length of the following rectangle is 9 centimeters and its width is 4 centimeters. What is the area of the rectangle?

A. 13 cm²

B. 26 cm²

C. 36 cm²

D. 48 cm²

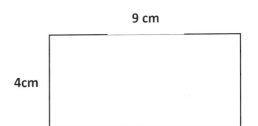

9) Look at the spinner above. On which color is the spinner most likely to land?

A. Red

B. Yellow

C. Green

D. None

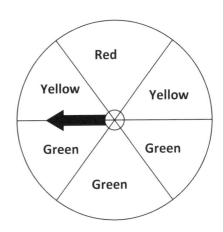

10) A group of third grade students recorded the following distances that they jumped.

11 inches	24 inches	12 inches	16 inches
24 inches	21 inches	13 inches	22 inches
20 inches	16 inches	12 inches	24 inches

What is the distance that was jumped most often?

A. 13

B. 11

C. 22

D. 24

Session 2

❖ **Calculators are NOT permitted for this practice test.**

❖ **Time for Session 2: 85 Minutes**

11) A number sentence such as $14 + Z = 32$ can be called an equation. If this equation is true, then which of the following equations is not true?

A. $32 - 14 = Z$

B. $32 - Z = 14$

C. $Z - 32 = 14$

D. $Z = 18$

12) Which number correctly completes the number sentence $30 \times 21 =$?

A. 261

B. 620

C. 360

D. 630

13) Which of the following statements describes the number 78,224?

A. The sum of seven thousands, 8 thousands, two hundreds, twenty tens, and four ones

B. The sum of seven thousands, 2 thousands, two hundreds, two tens, and four ones

C. The sum of seventy thousands, 2 thousands, two hundreds, twenty tens, and four ones

D. The sum of seventy thousands, 8 thousands, two hundreds, two tens, and four ones

14) Use the models below to answer the question.

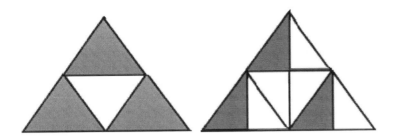

Which statement about the models is true?

A. Each shows the same fraction because they are the same size.

B. Each shows a different fraction because they are different shapes.

C. Each shows the same fraction because they both have 3 sections

shaded.

D. Each shows a different fraction because they both have 3 shaded

sections but a different number of total sections.

15) Classroom A contains 8 rows of chairs with 4 chairs per row. If classroom

B has three times as many chairs, which number sentence can be used to

find the number of chairs in classroom B?

A. $8 \times 4 + 3$

B. $8 + 4 \times 3$

C. $8 \times 4 \times 3$

D. $8 + 4 + 3$

16) Which number correctly completes the subtraction sentence

$$3,000 - 2,100 = \underline{\hspace{1cm}}?$$

A. 900

B. 1,100

C. 600

D. 800

17) A cafeteria menu had spaghetti with meatballs for $3 and bean soup for $5

How much would it cost to buy four plates of spaghetti with meatballs and

four bowls of bean soup?

Write your answer in the box below.

```



```

18) Emma flew 4,327 miles from Los Angeles to New York City. What is the

number of miles Emma flew rounded to the nearest thousand?

A. 4,500

B. 5,000

C. 4,300

D. 4,000

19) To what number is the arrow pointing?

A. 12

B. 8

C. 5

D. 6

20) Jason packs 14 boxes with flashcards. Each box holds 10 flashcards. How many flashcards Jason can pack into these boxes?

A. 40

B. 280

C. 310

D. 140

"This is the end of the practice test 5"

Georgia Milestones Assessment

System Practice Test 6

Mathematics

GRADE 3

Administered *Month Year*

Session 1

❖ **Calculators are NOT permitted for this practice test.**

❖ **Time for Session 1: 85 Minutes**

1) Kayla has 102 red cards and 78 white cards. How many more reds cards than white cards do Kayla have?

  A. 48

  B. 42

  C. 24

  D. 28

2) A number sentence is shown below.

  $4 \times 4 \square 3 = 48$

  What symbol goes into the box to make the number sentence true?

  A. $\times$

  B. $-$

  C. $+$

  D. $\div$

3) Liam had 220 marbles. Then, he gave 120 of the cards to his friend Ethan.

  After that, Liam lost 43 cards.

  Which equation can be used to find the number of cards Eve has now?

  A. $220 - 120 + 43 =$

  B. $220 - 120 - 43 =$

  C. $220 + 120 + 43 =$

  D. $220 + 120 - 43 =$

4) What is the value of "B" in the following equation?

$$44 + B + 21 = 82$$

A. 16

B. 27

C. 22

D. 17

5) There are two different cards on the table.

- There are 3 rows that have 15 red cards in each row.

- There are 16 white cards.

How many cards are there on the table?

A. 65

B. 61

C. 59

D. 71

6) Which of the following list shows only fractions that are equivalent to $\frac{1}{4}$?

A. $\frac{2}{8}, \frac{3}{12}, \frac{5}{20}$

B. $\frac{2}{16}, \frac{3}{12}, \frac{4}{20}$

C. $\frac{3}{12}, \frac{5}{16}, \frac{4}{20}$

D. $\frac{3}{12}, \frac{5}{16}, \frac{4}{20}$

7) What mixed number is shown by the shaded triangles?

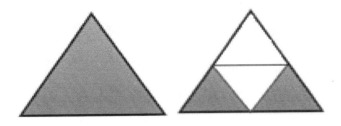

Write your answer in the box below.

8) Mason is 15 months now and he usually eats seven meals a day. How many meals does he eat in a week?

    A. 42

    B. 7

    C. 49

    D. 14

9) The perimeter of a square is 16 units. Each side of this square is the same length. What is the length of one side of the square in units?

    A. 10

    B. 2

    C. 6

    D. 4

10) Which of the following comparison of fractions is true?

A. $\frac{2}{4} = \frac{4}{8}$

B. $\frac{2}{4} > \frac{4}{8}$

C. $\frac{2}{4} < \frac{4}{8}$

D. $\frac{2}{4} < \frac{1}{4}$

Session 2

❖ **Calculators are NOT permitted for this practice test.**

❖ **Time for Session 2: 85 Minutes**

11) What is the perimeter of this rectangle?

A. 30 cm

B. 16 cm

C. 26 cm

D. 15 cm

5 cm

3 cm

12) Nicole has 3 quarters, 6 dimes, and 25 pennies. How much money does

Nicole have?

A. 150 pennies

B. 160 pennies

C. 120 pennies

D. 260 pennies

13) Noah packs 13 boxes with crayons. Each box holds 30 crayons. How many

crayons Noah can pack into these boxes?

A. 390

B. 590

C. 690

D. 330

14) There are 60 minutes in an hour. How many minutes are in 5 hours?

    A. 300 minutes

    B. 320 minutes

    C. 360 minutes

    D. 250 minutes

15) There are 8 rows of chairs in a classroom with 4 chairs in each row. How many chairs are in the classroom?

    A. 42

    B. 32

    C. 36

    D. 46

16) Which number correctly completes the number sentence $50 \times 17 = ?$

    A. 450

    B. 580

    C. 850

    D. 480

17) Michael has 576 marbles. What is this number rounded to the nearest ten?

Write your answer in the box below.

18) The sum of 7 ten thousand, 9 hundred, and 5 tens can be expressed as what number in standard form?

    A. 7,950

    B. 70,950

    C. 70,095

    D. 70,905

19) What is the perimeter of the following triangle?

    A. 24 inches

    B. 12 inches

    C. 21 inches

    D. 15 inches

4 inches   11 inches   6 inches

20) Moe has 280 cards. He wants to put them in boxes of 20 cards. How many boxes does he need?

    A. 10

    B. 28

    C. 7

    D. 14

"This is the end of practice test 6"

Answer Keys
Georgia Milestones Assessment System
Practice Tests

❋ Now, it's time to review your results to see where you went wrong and what areas you need to improve!

GMAS - Mathematics

Practice Test - 1				Practice Test - 2			
1	A	11	C	1	C	11	B
2	D	12	D	2	A	12	B
3	C	13	D	3	B	13	A
4	31	14	D	4	D	14	A
5	D	15	C	5	B	15	B
6	D	16	A	6	A	16	C
7	B	17	45	7	$2\frac{3}{4}$	17	850
8	C	18	D	8	C	18	B
9	C	19	B	9	D	19	C
10	D	20	D	10	A	20	D

GMAS - Mathematics

Practice Test - 3			
1	A	11	C
2	D	12	D
3	C	13	D
4	34	14	D
5	D	15	C
6	D	16	A
7	B	17	30
8	C	18	D
9	C	19	B
10	D	20	D

Practice Test - 4			
1	C	11	B
2	A	12	B
3	B	13	A
4	D	14	A
5	B	15	B
6	A	16	C
7	$2\frac{1}{4}$	17	960
8	C	18	B
9	D	19	C
10	A	20	D

GMAS - Mathematics

Practice Test - 5

1	A	11	C
2	D	12	D
3	C	13	D
4	41	14	D
5	D	15	C
6	D	16	A
7	B	17	32
8	C	18	D
9	C	19	B
10	D	20	D

Practice Test - 6

1	C	11	B
2	A	12	B
3	B	13	A
4	D	14	A
5	B	15	B
6	A	16	C
7	$1\frac{1}{2}$	17	580
8	C	18	B
9	D	19	C
10	A	20	D

Answers and

Explanations

Practice Test 1

Georgia Milestones Assessment

System - Mathematics

Answers and Explanations

1) Answer: A.

1 day: 24 hours

2 days = 2× 24 = 48 hours

2) Answer: D.

The clock shows 2:15 PM. One hour before that was 1:15 PM. 45 minutes

before that was 12:30 PM.

3) Answer: C.

The Football team buys 12 uniforms that each uniform cost $30. Therefore,

they should pay

(12 × $30 =) $360.

Choice C is the correct answer.

(30 × 10) + (30 × 2) = 300 + 60 = 360

4) Answer: 31.

Olivia wants to put 93 pastilles into boxes of 3 pastilles. Therefore, she

needs (93 ÷ 3 =) 31 boxes.

5) Answer: D.

Mia saved $46 and $38. Therefore, she has $84 now.

$160 - $84 = $76

She needs to save 76.

6) Answer: D.

Michelle puts 84 books in 4 boxes. Therefore, 84 ÷ 4 formula is correct.

7) Answer: B.

Elise gave 352 of her 956 cards to her friend. Therefore, she has 956 – 352 cards now. Then she lost 250 cards. Now, she has (956 – 352 – 250) = 354 cards

8) Answer: C.

Use area formula of a rectangle: Area = length × width

Area = 4cm × 9cm = 36 cm^2

9) Answer: C.

The chance of landing on yellow is 3 out of 6.

The chance of landing on red is 1 out of 6.

The chance of landing on green is 2 out of 6.

The chance of landing on yellow red is more than the chance of landing on other colors.

10)   Answer: D.

36 is the most frequent number in the table.

11)   Answer: C.

25 + Z = 92 Then, Z = (92 – 25=) 67.

All these equations are true:

92 – 25 = Z

92 – Z = 25

Z = 67

But this equation is not true: Z – 92 = 25

12)   Answer: D.

80 × 35 = 2,800

13)   Answer: D.

26,586 is the sum of:

20,000 + 6,000 + 500 + 80 + 6

14)   Answer: D.

The first model from left is divided into 4 equal parts. 3 out of 4 parts are shaded. The fraction for this model is $\frac{3}{4}$. The second model is divided into 8 equal parts. 3 out of 8 parts are shaded. Therefore, the fraction of the shaded parts for this model is $\frac{3}{8}$. These two models represent different fractions.

15)   Answer: C.

Classroom A contains 7 rows of chairs with four chairs per row. Therefore, there are $(7 \times 5 =)$ 35 chairs in Classroom A. Classroom B has three times as many chairs. Then, there are $(7 \times 5 \times 3)$ chairs in Classroom B.

16)   Answer: A.

$7,000 - 858 = 6,142$

17)   Answer: 45.

3 plates of spaghetti with meatballs cost: $3 \times \$8 = \$24$

3 bowls of bean soup cost: $3 \times \$7 = \$21$

3 plates of spaghetti with meatballs + 3 bowls of bean soup cost:

$\$24 + \$21 = \$45$

18)   Answer: D.

The number 3,391 rounded to the nearest thousand is 3,000.

19)   Answer: B.

The arrow shows a number between two numbers 20 and 36. $(36 - 20 = 16, 16 \div 2 = 8) \Rightarrow 20 + 8 = 28$

Therefore, the answer is 28.

20)   Answer: D.

To find the answer, multiply 12 by 30.

$12 \times 30 = 360$

Practice Test 2

Georgia Milestones Assessment

System - Mathematics

Answers and Explanations

1) Answer: C.

To find the answer subtract 88 from 109. The answer is $(120 - 85) = 35$.

2) Answer: A.

$3 \times 5 = 15$. Then: $3 \times 5 \;\square\; 8 = 120$

$15 \;\square\; 8 = 120 \Rightarrow 120 = 15 \times 8$

3) Answer: B.

Liam gave 432 of his marbles to his friend. Now he has $835 - 432 = 403$

He lost 116 of his marbles. Now, he has $403 - 116 = 287$ or

$(835 - 432 - 116)$.

4) Answer: D.

$43 + B + 7 = 63 \Rightarrow 50 + B = 63 \Rightarrow B = 63 - 50 = 13$

5) Answer: B.

3 rows that have 12 red cards in each row contain: $3 \times 12 = 36$ red cards

And there are 21 white cards on table. Therefore, there are $36 + 21 = 57$

cards on table.

6) Answer: A.

All these fractions; $\frac{3}{9}, \frac{5}{15}, \frac{24}{72}$ are equivalent to $\frac{1}{3}$.

7) Answer: $2\frac{3}{4}$.

This shape shows 2 complete shaded rectangle and 3 parts of a triangle

divided into 4 equal parts. It is equal to $2\frac{3}{4}$.

8) Answer: C.

If Mason eats 4 meals in 1 day, then, in a week (7days) he eats ($7 \times 4 = 28$) meals.

9) Answer: D.

Perimeter of the square is 32. Then:

$32 = 4 \times$ side $\Rightarrow$ side $= 8$

Each side of the square is 8 units.

10) Answer: A.

Simplify $\frac{9}{15}$ that's equal to $\frac{3}{5}$. Only option A is correct.

11) Answer: B.

Use perimeter of rectangle formula.

Perimeter $= 2 \times$ length $+ 2 \times$ width

$\Rightarrow$ P$= 2 \times 5 + 2 \times 7 = 10 + 14 = 24$ cm

12) Answer: B.

3 quarters $= 3 \times 25$ pennies $= 75$ pennies

5 dimes $= 5 \times 10$ pennies $= 50$ pennies

In total Nicole has 129 pennies

13) Answer: A.

$16 \times 30 = 480$

14) Answer: A.

1 hour $= 60$ minutes

5 hours $= 5 \times 60$ minutes $\Rightarrow$ 5hours $= 300$ minutes

15) Answer: B.

8 rows of chairs with 7 chairs in each row means: $8 \times 7 = 56$ chairs in total.

16) Answer: C.

$52 \times 14 = 728$

17) Answer: 850.

We round the number up to the nearest ten if the last digit in the number is 5, 6, 7, 8, or 9.

We round the number down to the nearest ten if the last digit in the number is 1, 2, 3, or 4.

If the last digit is 0, then we do not have to do any rounding, because it is already rounded to the ten.

Therefore, rounded number of 845 to the nearest ten is 850.

18) Answer: B.

4 ten thousand = 40,000

7 hundred = 700

8 tens = 80

Add all: 40,000 + 700 + 80 = 40,780

19) Answer: C.

To find the perimeter of the triangle, add all three sides.

Perimeter = 12 + 16 + 20 = 48 inches

20) Answer: D.

Moe wants to put 460 cards into boxes of 20 cards. Therefore, he needs (460 ÷ 20 =) 23 boxes.

Practice Test 3

Georgia Milestones Assessment

System - Mathematics

Answers and Explanations

1) Answer: A.

1 day: 24 hours

3 days = 3 × 24 = 72 hours

2) Answer: D.

The clock shows 2:15 PM. Three hour before that was 11:15 AM. 25

minutes before that was 10:50 AM.

3) Answer: C.

The Football team buys 14 uniforms that each uniform cost $20. Therefore,

they should pay

(14 × $20 =) $280.

Choice C is the correct answer.

(20 × 10) + (20 × 4) = 200 + 80 = 280

4) Answer: 34.

Olivia wants to put 136 pastilles into boxes of 4 pastilles. Therefore, she

needs (136 ÷ 4 =) 34 boxes.

5) Answer: D.

Mia saved $37 and $61. Therefore, she has $98 now.

$143 - $98 = $45

She needs to save 45.

6) Answer: D.

Michelle puts 65 books in 3 boxes. Therefore, 65 ÷ 3 formula is correct.

7) Answer: B.

Elise gave 328 of her 692 cards to her friend. Therefore, she has 692 – 328 cards now. Then she lost 213 cards. Now, she has (692 – 328 – 213) = 151 cards

8) Answer: C.

Use area formula of a rectangle: Area = length × width

Area = 5 cm × 7 cm = 35 cm²

9) Answer: C.

The chance of landing on red is 3 out of 6.

The chance of landing on green is 1 out of 6.

The chance of landing on yellow is 2 out of 6.

The chance of landing on red is more than the chance of landing on other colors.

10) Answer: D.

26 is the most frequent number in the table.

11) Answer: C.

31 + Z = 86 Then, Z = (86 – 31=) 55.

All these equations are true:

86 – 31 = Z

86 – Z = 31

Z = 55

But this equation is not true: Z – 86 = 31

12) Answer: D.

60 × 42 = 2,520

13) Answer: D.

63,425 is the sum of:

60,000 + 3,000 + 400 + 20 + 5

14) Answer: D.

The first model from left is divided into 4 equal parts. 1 out of 4 parts are shaded. The fraction for this model is $\frac{1}{4}$. The second model is divided into 8 equal parts. 1 out of 8 parts are shaded. Therefore, the fraction of the shaded parts for this model is $\frac{1}{8}$. These two models represent different fractions.

15) Answer: C.

Classroom A contains 9 rows of chairs with two chairs per row. Therefore, there are $(9 \times 6 =)$ 54 chairs in Classroom A. Classroom B has three times as many chairs. Then, there are $(9 \times 6 \times 2)$ chairs in Classroom B.

16) Answer: A.

$8,000 - 1,980 = 6,020$

17) Answer: 30.

2 plates of spaghetti with meatballs cost: $2 \times \$9 = \$18$

2 bowls of bean soup cost: $2 \times \$6 = \$12$

2 plates of spaghetti with meatballs + 2 bowls of bean soup cost:

$\$18 + \$12 = \$30$

18) Answer: D.

The number 7,293 rounded to the nearest thousand is 7,000.

19) Answer: B.

The arrow shows a number between two numbers 15 and 25. $(25 - 15 = 10, 10 \div 2 = 5) \Rightarrow 15 + 5 = 20$

Therefore, the answer is 20.

20) Answer: D.

To find the answer, multiply 24 by 15.

$24 \times 15 = 360$

Practice Test 4

Georgia Milestones Assessment

System - Mathematics

Answers and Explanations

1) Answer: C.

To find the answer subtract 95 from 155. The answer is $(155 - 95) = 60$.

2) Answer: A.

$6 \times 7 = 42$. Then: $6 \times 7 \square 5 = 210$

$42 \square 5 = 210 \Rightarrow 210 = 42 \times 5$

3) Answer: B.

Liam gave 241 of his marbles to his friend. Now he has $548 - 241 = 307$

He lost 86 of his marbles. Now, he has $307 - 86 = 221$ or

$(548 - 241 - 86)$.

4) Answer: D.

$38 + B + 16 = 77 \Rightarrow 54 + B = 77 \Rightarrow B = 77 - 54 = 23$

5) Answer: B.

5 rows that have 14 red cards in each row contain: $5 \times 14 = 70$ red cards

And there are 23 white cards on table. Therefore, there are $70 + 23 = 93$

cards on table.

6) Answer: A.

All these fractions; $\frac{3}{15}, \frac{5}{25}, \frac{24}{120}$ are equivalent to $\frac{1}{5}$.

7) Answer: $2\frac{1}{4}$.

This shape shows 2 complete shaded triangle and 1 parts of a triangle

divided into 4 equal parts. It is equal to $2\frac{1}{4}$.

8) Answer: C.

If Mason eats 2 meals in 1 day, then, in a week (7days) he eats ($7 \times 2 = 14$) meals.

9) Answer: D.

Perimeter of the square is 44. Then:

$44 = 4 \times \text{side} \Rightarrow \text{side} = 11$

Each side of the square is 11 units.

10) Answer: A.

Simplify $\frac{9}{24}$ that's equal to $\frac{3}{8}$. Only option A is correct.

11) Answer: B.

Use perimeter of rectangle formula.

Perimeter = $2 \times \text{length} + 2 \times \text{width}$

$\Rightarrow P = 2 \times 8 + 2 \times 10 = 16 + 20 = 36$ cm

12) Answer: B.

2 quarters = 2×25 pennies = 50 pennies

9 dimes = 9×10 pennies = 90 pennies

In total Nicole has 152 pennies

13) Answer: A.

$19 \times 20 = 380$

14) Answer: A.

1 hour = 60 minutes

4 hours = 4×60 minutes $\Rightarrow$ 4 hours = 240 minutes

15) Answer: B.

9 rows of chairs with 5 chairs in each row means: $9 \times 5 = 45$ chairs in total.

16) Answer: C.

$48 \times 15 = 720$

17) Answer: 960.

We round the number up to the nearest ten if the last digit in the number is 5, 6, 7, 8, or 9.

We round the number down to the nearest ten if the last digit in the number is 1, 2, 3, or 4.

If the last digit is 0, then we do not have to do any rounding, because it is already rounded to the ten.

Therefore, rounded number of 958 to the nearest ten is 960.

18) Answer: B.

5 ten thousand = 50,000

3 hundred = 300

4 tens = 40

Add all: 50,000 + 300 + 40 = 50,340

19) Answer: C.

To find the perimeter of the triangle, add all three sides.

Perimeter = 9 + 12 + 15 = 36 inches

20) Answer: D.

Moe wants to put 630 cards into boxes of 30 cards. Therefore, he needs ($630 \div 30 =$) 21 boxes.

Practice Test 5

Georgia Milestones Assessment

System - Mathematics

Answers and Explanations

1) Answer: A.

1 day: 24 hours

7 days = 7 × 24 = 168 hours

2) Answer: D.

The clock shows 8:15 PM. Four hour before that was 4:15 AM. 20 minutes before that was 3:55 PM.

3) Answer: C.

The Football team buys 11 uniforms that each uniform cost $30. Therefore, they should pay (11 × $30 =) $330.

Choice C is the correct answer.

(30 × 10) + (30 × 1) = 300 + 30 = 330

4) Answer: 41.

Olivia wants to put 82 pastilles into boxes of 2 pastilles. Therefore, she needs

(82 ÷ 2 =) 41 boxes.

5) Answer: D.

Mia saved $14 and $23. Therefore, she has $47 now.

$76 - $47 = $29

She needs to save 29.

6) Answer: D.

Michelle puts 45 books in 5 boxes. Therefore, 45 ÷ 5 formula is correct.

7) Answer: B.

Elise gave 54 of her 98 cards to her friend. Therefore, she has 98 – 54 cards now. Then she lost 13 cards. Now, she has (98 – 54 – 13) = 31 cards

8) Answer: C.

Use area formula of a rectangle: Area = length × width

Area = 4cm × 9cm = 36 cm^2

9) Answer: C.

The chance of landing on yellow is 2 out of 6.

The chance of landing on red is 1 out of 6.

The chance of landing on green is 3 out of 6.

The chance of landing on green is more than the chance of landing on other colors.

10) Answer: D.

24 is the most frequent number in the table.

11) Answer: C.

14 + Z = 32 Then, Z = (32 – 14=) 18.

All these equations are true:

32 – 14 = Z

32 – Z = 14

Z = 18

But this equation is not true: Z – 32 = 14

12) Answer: D.

30 × 21 = 630

13) Answer: D.

78,224 is the sum of:

70,000 + 8,000 + 200 + 20 + 4

14) Answer: D.

The first model from left is divided into 4 equal parts. 3 out of 4 parts are shaded. The fraction for this model is $\frac{3}{4}$. The second model is divided into 8 equal parts. 3 out of 8 parts are shaded. Therefore, the fraction of the shaded parts for this model is $\frac{3}{8}$. These two models represent different fractions.

15) Answer: C.

Classroom A contains 8 rows of chairs with four chairs per row. Therefore, there are $(8 \times 4 =)$ 32 chairs in Classroom A. Classroom B has three times as many chairs. Then, there are $(8 \times 4 \times 3)$ chairs in Classroom B.

16) Answer: A.

$3,000 - 2,100 = 900$

17) Answer: 32.

4 plates of spaghetti with meatballs cost: $4 \times \$3 = \$12$

4 bowls of bean soup cost: $4 \times \$5 = \$20$

4 plates of spaghetti with meatballs + 4 bowls of bean soup cost:

$\$12 + \$20 = \$32$

18) Answer: D.

The number 4,327 rounded to the nearest thousand is 4,000.

19) Answer: B.

The arrow shows a number between two numbers 3 and 13. $(13 - 3 = 10, 10 \div 2 = 5) \Longrightarrow 3 + 5 = 8$

Therefore, the answer is 8.

20) Answer: D.

To find the answer, multiply 14 by 10.

$14 \times 10 = 140$

Practice Test 6

Georgia Milestones Assessment

System - Mathematics

Answers and Explanations

1) Answer: C.

To find the answer subtract 78 from 102. The answer is $(102 - 78) = 24$.

2) Answer: A.

$4 \times 4 = 16$. Then: $4 \times 4 \; \square \; 3 = 48$

$16 \; \square \; 3 = 48 \Rightarrow 48 = 16 \times 3$

3) Answer: B.

Liam gave 120 of his marbles to his friend. Now he has $220 - 120 = 100$

He lost 43 of his marbles. Now, he has $100 - 43 = 57$ or

$(220 - 120 - 43)$.

4) Answer: D.

$44 + B + 21 = 82 \Rightarrow 65 + B = 82 \Rightarrow B = 82 - 65 = 17$

5) Answer: B.

3 rows that have 15 red cards in each row contain: $3 \times 15 = 45$ red cards

And there are 16 white cards on table. Therefore, there are $45 + 16 = 61$

cards on table.

6) Answer: A.

All these fractions; $\frac{2}{8}, \frac{3}{12}, \frac{5}{20}$ are equivalent to $\frac{1}{4}$.

7) Answer: $1\frac{1}{2}$.

This shape shows 1 complete shaded triangle and 2 parts of a triangle

divided into 4 equal parts. It is equal to $1\frac{2}{4} = 1\frac{1}{2}$.

8) Answer: C.

If Mason eats 7 meals in 1 day, then, in a week (7days) he eats ($7 \times 7 = 49$) meals.

9) Answer: D.

Perimeter of the square is 16. Then:

$16 = 4 \times$ side $\Rightarrow$ side $= 4$

Each side of the square is 4 units.

10) Answer: A.

Simplify $\frac{4}{8}$ that's equal to $\frac{2}{4}$. Only option A is correct.

11) Answer: B.

Use perimeter of rectangle formula.

Perimeter $= 2 \times$ length $+ 2 \times$ width

$\Rightarrow$ P= $2 \times 3 + 2 \times 5 = 6 + 10 = 16$ cm

12) Answer: B.

3 quarters $= 3 \times 25$ pennies $= 75$ pennies

6 dimes $= 6 \times 10$ pennies $= 60$ pennies

In total Nicole has 160 pennies

13) Answer: A.

$13 \times 30 = 390$

14) Answer: A.

1 hour = 60 minutes

5 hours $= 5 \times 60$ minutes $\Rightarrow$ 5 hours $= 300$ minutes

15) Answer: B.

8 rows of chairs with 4 chairs in each row means: $8 \times 4 = 32$ chairs in total.

16) Answer: C.

$50 \times 17 = 850$

17) Answer: 580.

We round the number up to the nearest ten if the last digit in the number is 5, 6, 7, 8, or 9.

We round the number down to the nearest ten if the last digit in the number is 1, 2, 3, or 4.

If the last digit is 0, then we do not have to do any rounding, because it is already rounded to the ten.

Therefore, rounded number of 576 to the nearest ten is 580.

18) Answer: B.

7 ten thousand = 70,000

9 hundred = 900

5 tens = 50

Add all: 70,000 + 900 + 50 = 70,950

19) Answer: C.

To find the perimeter of the triangle, add all three sides.

Perimeter = 4 + 6 + 11 = 21 inches

20) Answer: D.

Moe wants to put 280 cards into boxes of 20 cards. Therefore, he needs (280 ÷ 20 =) 14 boxes.

"End"

Made in the USA
Columbia, SC
12 May 2022

60353003R00059